Stop Embarrassing Yourself:

The Guide to Dining Etiquette

Leontina Richardson, MBA

Certified Corporate Etiquette and International
Protocol Consultant

Stop Embarrassing Yourself: The Guide to Dining Etiquette by Leontina Richardson, MBA

www.steppingintoetiquette.com

info@steppingintoetiquette.com

Dedication

I dedicate this book to my parents,
Cynthia and Stephen.

I could never have done this without your faith, support,
and constant encouragement.

To my angel in heaven, Rev. Willie F. Jordan Sr., thank
you for watching over me.

CONTENTS

Introduction

For the purposes of clarifying any misconceptions which the title of this book may cause one to interpret in a negative way, this introduction seeks to expound on the true and intentional meaning of the title in hopes of giving you a better understanding of this concept. Let me first start by defining the word etiquette. According to Vocabulary.com the term has been perfectly worded by stating that "Etiquette is a code of polite conduct. If you practice proper etiquette, you are less likely to offend or annoy people- and you may even charm them. Many people think etiquette is about table manners in fancy restaurants, but quite simply, it is expected behavior that shows respect, meant to make everyone feel comfortable."

With that being said, it is not necessary to think that one has a duty to proper etiquette only when dining in exquisite places. This is a general requirement for all dining activities, so as to avoid risking embarrassment of yourself and your dinner party. For example, when dining in public some individuals think that chewing with their mouths wide-open is acceptable, but believe it or not people in surrounding areas are generally watching, and to the dislike of many it is probably both distracting and annoying.

For the individual who engages in these acts, there is no doubt that coming to the realization that individuals around you are staring and probably whispering would be embarrassing to anyone in such a situation. As such, the title of this book is not purposed to bring to light the mistakes which you have made, but to showcase how common these errors are and to provide direction on how to better navigate the dining experience in a comfortable and confident manner.

In closing, don't take the title too seriously; it's merely a way to captivate your attention and to inspire you to grow into your best self. So now that we've got that out of the way, go forward in hopes of embracing this journey of learning how to apply dining etiquette to your daily life.

Where It All Started...

In the beginning, God created the heavens and the earth. Little did he know that the fashionable and talented humans whom he so gracefully mended didn't have the slightest clue of how to use silverware. Their eating habits were atrocious and despicable to watch, but being the great God of all things, He channeled His inner knowledge and scavenged through His brilliant ideas. After much thought and consideration He blessed me with the understanding to write this book for you!

Today marks the last day you'll get dressed in that amazing frock of yours and attend a beautiful wedding hosted by close friends and be halted by the arrangement of cutlery and dinnerware that petrifies you to death! If we're being honest, we've all experienced not just the fear of interacting with undesirable people who we've been paired with at the table, but also minor inanimate objects like forks and knives and stuff!

This book is a dining etiquette guide that will explore the errors and unforgettable mistakes we have all committed at one point or another. It will give you a renewed sense of self and banish those cringe-worthy memories that haunt us many times we sit down to have a meal in public. And while this guide is completely comprehensive, it isn't necessary that you absorb all of its awesomeness in a single serving. It may be effective to pinpoint topics that are relevant to important occasions. If you are going to a dinner party, skip to the chapter that addresses dinner party etiquette and learn to be a gracious guest. If you are going to a wedding, jump to the chapter on place settings and quickly skim the diagrams to make sure you don't drink from the wrong glass. So there is no need to memorize everything at once, just be certain to keep the book handy!

To maximize the effectiveness of this guide, be sure to follow these tips:

1. Read each section carefully, and then read it again!

2. While reading, you may casually fall upon some points that strike a nerve, for the last time, FORGIVE YOURSELF! There is a reason you got this book and are reading it right now--I've got you.

3. The information in this book is based on the American dining experience and may not be applicable in other countries. Be sure to research the cultural norms which are practiced in other countries you intend to visit to avoid misunderstandings.

4. Becoming well-versed in dining etiquette will require lots of practice, not just reading. Try to practice the things you learn at home before

heading out to that five star restaurant you drool about.

5. Give yourself time; practice becomes permanent.

It is important to note that the guidance which this book gives regarding dining etiquette isn't and shouldn't be limited to five star restaurants and formal settings. These tips also apply to informal dining in places such as fast food restaurants and casual eateries. In light of this, it is key to remember that this book entails quite a bit of information; so don't beat yourself up over not remembering it all in one read.

This book contains a little humor to lessen the harshness of a rather intimidating topic. Bear in mind that this is not intended to insult or bully you in any way, shape or form; its purpose is to facilitate an easier transition into becoming your best cutlery-using self. Lighten up and go with the flow, this is to help mend you, not break you. So let's get a move on! Next to be discussed is meeting the maître d' and the making of reservations.

Meeting the Maître D' and Making Reservations

Greeting the Maître D'

One of the first persons you will come into contact with when you enter a restaurant is the host or hostess, otherwise known as the maître d'. This is the individual who is tasked with providing you with comfortable and appropriate seating, whether or not reservations were made. One observation that I have made, which is utterly rude and distasteful, are individuals who barge into establishments demanding to be seated immediately without acknowledging the presence of the maître d'. It takes much more muscles to frown than it does to smile, so grab yourself a mirror and practice the formation of the curve! The next time you see a maître d' be sure to flash that whip of a smile and say hello; don't be a sour puss.

If in fact you didn't make reservations in advance, you might be asked to place your name and requested seating arrangements on a list, which might be lengthy. Try not to be antsy and short-tempered; this will only exasperate the situation and enrage waiting diners. Another revolting habit observed with some diners is the ill-conceived thought that every single person you are dining with needs to join the line to request seating. Let's just be logical for a moment, your one and a half year old probably can't even write his own name; leave all the children, parents, and other relatives and friends in the waiting area when submitting requests for seating. After all, it will permit the process to run more smoothly and without the added stress of keeping track of children and other fiduciaries. So, be sure to do a head count before you get out of the car.

After you have submitted your name and number of guests, do not by any means hover over the host as if you are attempting to inhale his carbon dioxide! Give the host some room and allow other diners to make their submissions. One way of knowing whether you are too close to the host's stand is if others inquire: "Are you in the line?" or "Where does the line start?" These are clues that you need to step away from the stand; perhaps you should return to check on your party.

If you are hosting a dinner party at a restaurant, it is your duty to arrive at the restaurant before your guests. It is the norm for hosts to await their guests in the foyer of the restaurant or at the table. Both are acceptable! However, if you choose the latter be sure to advise the maître d' of the fact that you are expecting other guests. A general description of their appearance would be beneficial to help the host direct them to your table.

If some of your guests have gathered in the foyer to wait for others and ten minutes have passed, ask the maître d' to seat your group and show the others to your table upon arrival.

Next we will proceed to discuss the formalities associated with making reservations.

Making Reservations

Making reservations in advance is definitely one of the best ways to avoid crowds and confusion when you decide to dine out. In the event that the spot and the day you wish to visit is popular among locals, do yourself a BIG favor and just call in advance to secure a reservation.

As a woman who definitely likes to go out looking fabulous, I always appreciate when dinner reservations are made ahead of time by the host, so as to prevent my toes enduring the gruesome pain from having to stand for an hour in four inch heels. Some guys may not understand where I'm coming from, but standing in an overcrowded foyer for an extended period of time is uncomfortable to say the least, especially in the colder months when attire is layered to prevent us from freezing.

While on the phone with the reservationist, you may also request a particular area or type of seating which is most suitable for your party. So, how exactly do you do this?

1. Call anywhere from two weeks to a day ahead (depending on the popularity of the restaurant) to reserve your spot.

2. If you are familiar with the restaurant and you prefer a certain section, let the reservationist know when you call.

3. Reconfirm your reservation on the day you wish to visit. There is probably nothing more distasteful that getting all dressed up and spending and hour on your makeup, only to have fast food for dinner because there was no reservation after all. You'll probably even want to go through the drive-thru section considering how overdressed you probably will be.

Chivalry First!

The following tips are for guys who desire to impress the ladies they dine with. This maneuver requires more effort and finesse if you intend to give the true treatment of a gentleman. After your table has been prepared and your group named has been called you will be asked to follow the maître d'. Here are some good suggestions to follow to help you put your best foot forward:

- Ladies First - One of the primary rules in this situation is that ladies should always be allowed to go first! Yes, no matter how long you have been waiting and the fact that your stomach is churning dust, get over the arousal of your senses by the delightful atmospheric smell and restrain yourself.

- Again, ladies first - In the event that the party contains a mixture of men and women, all the women should be allowed to go to the table before all of the men.

- And Again, ladies first - Upon reaching the table, women should be seated before men and by the men.

Frequently Asked Questions

Question: Can I request to be seated elsewhere if I have been seated in close proximity to an undesirable area such as a heavily trafficked place, the kitchen, or restroom?

Answer: Dining out should be an enjoyable experience. In the event that you are uncomfortable with the current condition of your seating arrangements, feel free to politely say, "May we please be seated at a less trafficked area?" There is no need to become loud and vulgar. Chances are the maître d' didn't intentionally seat you at the most undesirable spot in the entire restaurant because he didn't like the color of your shirt. Furthermore, in the event that you desired to sit in a booth, as opposed to other options, be sure to specify this to the maître d' prior to being escorted to your seat.

Question: I go to dinner with friends often and there's always 1-2 people who are always late. Do we have to wait for them to arrive before we order drinks and food?

Answer: No, you do not have to wait for the late guests to arrive before ordering drinks. Once seated, the punctual guests are allowed to order drinks and examine the menu for imminent ordering. After waiting another 15-20 minutes for the late guests, the group should proceed to order their meals.

Now we will dive into formal and informal place settings, along with the etiquette rules associated with each area to establish a clearer understanding of what's appropriate and inappropriate.

Understanding Place Settings

Generally, one of the most intimidating aspects of dining out is confronting a place setting that's well dressed with numerous spoons, forks, and knives, which you are completely clueless about how to use. In our own little world, there would probably just be one spoon, knife, and fork used for everything so as to exclude this nerve-wracking experience; and for many who will read this book, place settings will most definitely be one of the primary etiquette issues which they will seek to rectify. So without further ado, please familiarize yourself with the informal and formal place settings pictured below. You can do this! The diagrams may seem a bit more menacing than it truly is, but in no time I'm sure that you'll be instructing others on the appropriate use of these not so scary utensils! Please note, this is an "American Style" place setting.

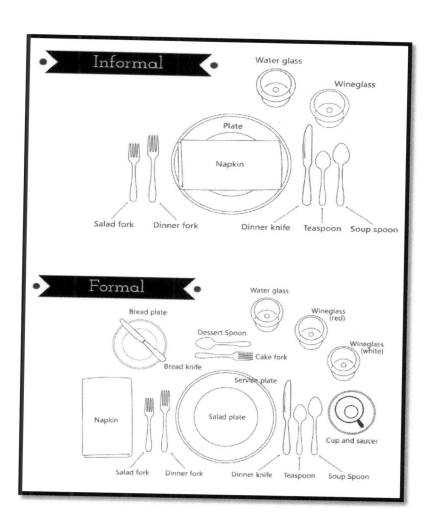

Now, what I am about to reveal to you is simply ingenious and I promise that you will absolutely, never, ever forget where the butter dish and your drinking glass should be positioned for the rest of your life! I guarantee! Simply open both hands, palms facing downward and try to touch the tip of your index finger on both hands with your thumbs. After doing this, you will realize that the fingers on your left hand form a "b", while the same on your right had form a "d", be patient and wait for what I'm getting at here. . The "b" on your left hand stands for bread plate, and the "d" on your right hand stands for drink. Your bread plate will always be to your left, and you glass will always be to the right of your plate. Isn't that just genius? This rule applies for both formal and informal settings.

Now we will briefly look at informal place settings.

Informal Place Settings
One of the best ways to remember where to put what is by simply remembering the notion that utensils are placed from the outside to the inside, as the diner will use the outermost pieces which lie furthest from the place at the beginning of the dining experience.

Think of a three-course meal for instance, the plate is the central and most essential part of the arrangement and the premise upon which all other utensils become necessary. So, placing the plate down first, place the salad fork to the outermost left of the plate – because the salad is served first, and the entree fork on the inside of the salad fork, closer to the plate. For the right side, the soup spoon will always be on the outside because it's served before the entrée. Always remember, this, "start from the outside, and work your way towards the plate". If you are setting the table, the sharp edge of your knife should face the right side of the plate.

Apart from the bread and butter plate and the wine glasses which were previously mentioned, a three-course setting may require the presence of a salad plate. In such a case, the salad plate is positioned to the left of the outermost fork. When coffee is served, the saucer and tea cup will be to the outermost right of the soup spoon.

Formal Place Settings

So, if you're in the mood for experiencing one of those major headaches, read on! Just joking, but you might really need to put on your thinking cap to completely grasp the positions of utensils in this place setting, so that you can go ahead and throw yourself one of those fancy formal dinners that would surely wow your guests.

First to be addressed is the charger, this is a large service plate which every course (except the dessert!) rests on. Charger plates have many practical purposes, besides the fact that they provide elegance and enhance the table setting's décor. Not only do they anchor the dining table, create ambiance, and are aesthetically pleasing to guests, chargers also protect the table and tablecloth from becoming dirty during service. Charger plates can catch pieces of food, and prevent spills and messes that would otherwise stain the tablecloth or flow onto the table. If you ever host a dinner party and want to be a bit fancy, make sure you follow these specific etiquette rules when using charger plates:

- Charger plates should always be dressed and ready when guests arrive.

- Chargers are always removed from the table after all guests are finished eating the main entrée.

- Chargers are never used when serving dessert.

- Chargers can be removed once all guests are seated, or they may remain on the table throughout the entire length of the meal.

- Place charger plates one inch away from the bottom edge of the table to create perfect alignment.

- Never serve food directly on top of a charger plate, unless it is coated in a food-safe material.

As with the previously mentioned main course, everything in the formal place setting remains the same, except in the instances where some specified food items will be served which require specific utensils. Foods which employ the use of special utensils include: oysters and fish. Regardless of their rare use, each implement still has a specific place on the formal place setting. These are as follows: the oyster fork goes to the right of the spoons, which as previously mentioned are located to the left of the charger/plate; the fish knife is positioned to the left of the dinner knife, which is located to the immediate right of the charger/plate; and the fish fork is placed to the left of the dinner fork. If the fish is served after the salad, it should be placed in between the salad and dinner fork.

At any one time, there may be a total number of five glasses present per place setting. An easy way of remembering their order and positioning may be to remember that the water goblet is located directly above the knives, then located to its right is the champagne flute, a red wine glass, a white wine glass and lastly, a sherry glass.

In the event that you forget the order of the utensils and which ones should be used at the appropriate time, the first thing you need to do is to stay calm then proceed to discretely observe others around you and act accordingly.

Napkin Etiquette

So now, you are finally seated and excited to indulge in a delightful meal..... just hold your brakes right there! The first thing that should flood your mind as soon as you are seated is "where is my napkin?" Who would've thought that such a tiny addition to the entire dining experience would have "etiquette rules"? Well, not to disturb your appetite, but you would be shocked at some of the abominations that napkins have endured over the years of their existence. It would only be fair to respect the nature and purpose of napkins by revealing how they should actually be used, especially in public.

Key facts on appropriate napkin use:

- The first thing you should do as soon as you sit is to place your napkin in your lap! Yes, even before you glance at the menu or begin ordering drinks. Don't shake, snap, or flash your napkin open under any circumstance. For crying out loud, we are not washing or hanging clothes!

- Large napkins are usually unfolded halfway, while smaller napkins are unfolded completely and cover the lap fully. Never, and I mean NEVER wear your napkin as a bib. If you are worried about wasting something on your clothes, you should consider sitting closer to the table.

- If ever you decide to excuse yourself from the table, your napkin should be placed on your chair.

- When you are done eating, and possibly about to leave, your napkin should be placed to the left of your plate. In the event that your plate has been removed, place your napkin where your plate was previously positioned.

- If your napkin drops under the table, do not pick it up. Discreetly ask your server for another napkin.

- You should always dab your mouth with your napkin, but for the sake of preserving the dignity of humanity, please don't use your napkin to overly wipe your face.

- The only time that you should actually wait to place your napkin in your lap is, if for instance you are at a dinner party. It is imperative that you wait for the host to initiate the dining experience before you place your napkin on your lap and begin to indulge.

Frequently Asked Questions

Question: I was out with someone and they asked the server for a black napkin. What's the purpose of a black napkin?

Answer: The purpose of a black napkin is to make sure that you do not get lint on your outfit if you are wearing dark bottoms.

Let's just say that asking for a black napkin is one thing that you definitely can do to boost your confidence and impress your guests. This most definitely will make you seem well experienced in the fabulous art of dining.

Question: I've been putting my napkin on my plate after meals for a couple of years now, are you really meaning to tell me that I've been doing it wrong all along?

Answer: Yes, that's exactly what I'm telling you! Imagine you had ordered a tender and delicious barbecue rotisserie chicken with mash potatoes on the side. When you are done with your meal, you will obviously have barbecue sauce and other stuff left on your plate. Do you really think it's a good idea to put a white cloth napkin on that plate? Absolutely not!

Basic Table Manners

Let's just think about the origins of table manners for a second. Someone must have been completely grossed out by the unsightly eating habits of other individuals and decided to take it upon themselves to begin the creation of what is now known as table manners. In consideration of this, we will now explore some of the things that you should never, ever do around the table! Remember that these table manners apply all across the board so whether you're dining with a great prince in Dubai or just having a potluck with your grandma's book club!

Points to Remember:

- Always chew with your mouth closed, and never talk while chewing food. This is simply a recipe for disaster and saliva! Smacking and slurping food are major mistakes and a sign of extremely bad table manners. Save yourself the stares and embarrassment by just conforming to the requirements of eating out.

- Savor the meal and eat slowly; it encourages conversation and hospitality. Nobody wants to go out to dinner with a person that just keeps shoveling heaps of food down their throat as if they haven't eaten in 25 years. Dining out isn't just about eating a meal; it essentially entails enjoying the company of friends and family over a delightful meal. So take the time to catch up with others over a nice meal.

- Place all electronic devices on silent or vibrate before entering the restaurant. If you forgot to turn off your cell phone and it rings, immediately turn it off. Do not answer the call. Do not text or browse the Internet while at the table with guests.

- Please don't use your utensils like some sort of medieval instrument you are using to catch the prey on your plate--no shoveling or stabbing.

- Do not hunch your shoulders over your plate. Apart from probably hurting yourself, it definitely looks funny! Likewise, slouching back in your chair (which makes it look as if you're not interested in the meal) is bad table manners and may even offend the host who invited you to dinner.

- Avoid picking food out of your teeth at the table with utensils. That is a definite turn off and is likely to cause a loss of appetite to all guests observing those actions.

- Remember to use your napkin to wipe your mouth and surrounding areas during and after eating. Forget using it on places like your forehead and other places where food definitely shouldn't be present.

- Never take a sip of your drink with food in your mouth. However, if you are choking, completely disregard this tip and drink from the water pitcher if you need to!

- Never place your elbows on the table while you are eating. If you are in between courses, you can rest your elbows on the table.

- Never reach in front of a fellow diner for something; politely ask someone to pass the item to you. And remember, always say please and thank you.

- When sneezing or coughing at the table is unavoidable, cover your nose or mouth with a napkin and proceed as quietly as possible. Except in an emergency when you feel that monster sneeze barreling down your nostrils, don't use a napkin to blow your nose. Act quickly and leave the table and use a handkerchief instead.

- Do not gesture with a knife or fork in your hands when speaking to other guests around the table. Not only is it creepy, you could actually injure someone without any intention of doing so. Let's not turn this amazing meal into an accident scene, gesture with hands only!

- A lady should refrain from replenishing lipstick before coming to the table. This is to prevent an imprint of lipstick on the rim of a glass or a napkin. We definitely don't want red lipstick plastered everywhere! A little trick which can be done to prevent this is by taking a ply of tissue and placing it between both lips, pressing down. This should remove the lipstick that is on the underside of the lip.

- Each time service is provided at a multi-course meal, verbal acceptance is not necessary. However, in order to refuse service, a verbal rejection of "No, thank you," is given. At a simple meal when a serving bowl is passed upon request, say "Thank you." Manners are extremely important while dining. Don't be that person that is completely caught up in the food that simply forgets all their manners.

Okay, now that we've gotten that out of the way I know you're anxious to hear about the actual eating process, so here it goes.....

Let's Order

Congratulations for making it to the next step of your etiquette journey! By now you should feel like an authentic dining samurai.... Wait, that sounds a bit too aggressive, let's go with guru, dining guru; so give yourself a good pat on the shoulder for effort. However, you're not quite there yet young grasshopper--let's just say you're about 40% there.

Having covered place settings and napkin etiquette, it's now time to order!

Not many individuals are of the awareness that ordering meals in a restaurant environment employs a certain level and aptitude of deportment. Simply put, there are actually right and wrong ways to order your meals and converse with the server. In this chapter, those intricacies will be explored, and the professional diner in you will boldly emerge. It is also essential to know what is acceptable when dining with guests.

I know that this isn't a job interview or business etiquette guide, I really do get it; but in your best interest and for the maintenance of my sanity, let us discuss how to order while dining with a potential employer or even at a business function when you aren't actually paying for the meal.

Quite a number of business interactions and job interviews may take place during lunch or dinner and the way that we order and the quantity of the order will tell your prospective employer quite a bit about your character. What I'm actually trying to say is, please don't attempt to order the entire menu and then proceed to force feed yourself all in one sitting. This not only deters the potential employer, it would leave a very bad self-representation. One trick for finding out what your host might order is to ask them what they like or whether they have a favorite dish. For the love of etiquette, it is extremely distasteful to purchase the most expensive item on the menu, but it wouldn't do you much good to order the cheapest one either. Instead, opt for a dish that is priced mid-range that you would actually eat.

Furthermore, you certainly do not want to order three courses when you are not paying. Yes, it is essential for you to feel comfortable but that comfort doesn't have to come from the food you are about to order. Get comfortable by engaging in light conversation such as sharing interests and goals.

Here are a couple more tips that I strongly believe you will find useful when dining with someone who is paying the bill:

- Do not under any circumstance experiment with new food. This avoids the chance of you disliking the food and having to pick around the food throughout the meal.

- Follow the lead of your companion. If your host doesn't order an appetizer, you shouldn't either. You probably won't like this rule, but what will actually happen is that you ordering an appetizer will prolong the time that the host will receive their entree.

Restaurant Ordering Sequence

How to order will depend upon whether you're the host or guest, how many people are at the table, and whether the guests are male or female. The host is the person that will be paying the check; his/her order is generally taken last. In a group, the server may decide how the ordering will proceed. Normally, women are allowed to place their orders first. Gentlemen, if you are dining with a lady, she should always place her order first – no exceptions!

Communicating with the Server

Although it is the responsibility of the server to take your order, deliver your meals, and ensure that all is well with your party, it is important to remember that they are real people, living real lives, and experiencing real emotions. I'm in no way suggesting that you and the server should become best buds, but a certain level of respect and professionalism is expected to be demonstrated. Follow these important tips as it relates to communicating with your server:

- When you are talking to your server, it is important to maintain proper eye contact, even while ordering your food and drinks. This clearly demonstrates to the server that you value and respect them.

- To get your servers attention, it is extremely rude to wave at them from across the room. Don't do that. They make rounds to check on you regularly; just be patient and wait!

- Oftentimes servers stay away from tables when they observe that most of the guests are still flipping through the menu. The best way to show that you are ready to order and to gain your servers attention is to close the menu. You'd be surprised at how quickly you are approached.

- The server will always serve food from your left and beverages from your right side. Keep this in mind to know which beverages are yours. We don't want to sip on someone else's wine, now do we?

- Lastly, before you proceed to order, ensure that you know what you want to order and that everyone at the table is ready to place their orders.

Beverage Etiquette

So you've finally placed your order and the thirst is upon you. It feels like the Sahara desert uprooted and became implanted in the depths of your mouth!

Beverages are generally the first items that are brought to the table once you have been seated. Surprisingly, there are beverage etiquette rules that you should follow while dining with others. Yes, that may sound ridiculous, but it's true! Have you ever dined with someone who squirted lemons in their water and then put the lemon on the table after use? I've seen this so many times which is why I thought it would be appropriate to have a chapter on beverage etiquette.

Here are a few beverage etiquette tips to consider when ordering specifics drinks:

Water or Soft Drinks

- It is ok to ask for a straw for your water.

- If you choose to put lemons in your water, cup your free hand (which is assumedly clean) over the lemon and gently squeeze the fruit.

- If you have ice in your water, never crunch the ice in your mouth; this also applies to if you are drinking a soft drink.

- Never drink from your glass when you have food in your mouth. You don't want food particles floating in your water, do you?

- Don't gulp, take sips.

- Women, go easy on the lipstick to make sure your glass isn't smudged with lipstick around the rim.

Wine

There is quite a bit of information on the art of wine handling and drinking that extends beyond this book. The purpose of this section is to give you a general idea of how to conduct yourself during the dining experience when wine is served. The following are tips for the correct way to hold wine glasses:

- White wine glasses are held by the stem, not the bowl as it is served chilled and the body heat passing through your hands may alter its temperature, and in some case its flavor.

- Red wine glasses may be held by the bowl as it is served at room temperature.

- Champagne flutes are held at the stem.

Coffee and Tea

Please keep in mind that coffee and tea are served at the end of the meal. Here are a few tips:

43

- Never leave your spoon in the coffee cup or teacup, you should always place it on the saucer or a plate.

- If your coffee or tea is scorching hot, never take ice from your water glass and put it in your hot beverage to cool it off.

- I know it looks quite fancy, but never hold up your pinky finger.

- Be sure to hold the tea cup or mug by the handle, please don't grasp the cup from the top and try to drink in that position. Apart from the fact that you will risk the possibility of burning yourself, you'll probably end up slurping, which is equally unpleasant.

Frequently Asked Question

Question: I use a lot of sugar packets in my coffee and I'm always so embarrassed because next to my saucer is always 8-10 packets. Is there another way to hide the empty packets?

Answer: You could put the empty packets in your pocket (or purse if you have one), but I don't recommend that. When dealing with empty packets of sugar or small containers of cream, you should crumple them and place them on the edge of your butter plate or saucer. Another important point is that you should not under any circumstances rip the wrapper open with your mouth! No ma'am!

The Art of Eating Breads, Soups, and Salads

Here we will get down to the intricacies of eating bread, soup, and salad, and a fervent discussion of which mannerisms are acceptable, and those areas that are less than desirable. We all know that excitement, laughter and good food go well together. However, there are some instances where the magnitude of these behaviors can be disruptive! Let's face it, who wants to sit next to someone that slurps their soup every time they bring their spoon to their mouth? In short, no one does because it's incredibly annoying.

Breaking Bread

Bread is served before the meal arrives to the table. It allows the diners to have a quick munch over conversation before their salad, soup, or main course. Most restaurants will either provide you with bread rolls or a complete loaf, and whether you believe it or not, there are specific ways in which both should be eaten. This is a very popular dish which is often eaten improperly, and although it seems easier and makes sense to slice the bread in two and butter it so that you don't have to constantly break and butter the bread, that style of eating is improper.

Below are the steps that you should follow when served a dinner roll:

1. Ask for the butter platter (sometimes the butter might be provided in a wrapper).

2. With the use of the butter knife that may be on the platter (if not, use your own knife) place just enough butter for your roll on your bread plate. You will butter your bread from your bread plate.

3. When you pass the bread basket, be sure to only touch the dinner roll that you want. If you are the first to pick up the bread basket, always offer to your left first and then pass to your right.

4. Break off a bite-sized piece of your bread.

5. With your knife, butter that piece. Never butter your roll or slice of bread all at once.

6. Place your knife on your bread plate (at the top) with the blade facing in.

7. Eat that bite-sized piece.

8. Repeat steps 4-7

In the event that your table is presented with an entire loaf of bread, the correct approach is to cut the bread into slices by use of the (usually) accompanying bread knife in one hand and a napkin used to reinforce the loaf in the other. You may start by cutting the loaf in half and slicing from one half as needed.

Frequently Asked Questions

Question: What happens when someone takes my bread plate?

Answer: Don't mention it to the person. The best thing to do is to put your bread on your dinner plate and then ask your server for a bread plate when he comes around.

Question: Is sopping with bread allowed?

Answer: To the surprise of many, you can actually sop your food with bread while dining in a restaurant. However, it most certainly must be done in a particular way! Extra gravy and sauces are the only items which you should ever consider sopping; attempting to sop anything else is definitely an offence under dining etiquette laws. This should be done by placing a piece of bread on the end of a fork, allow the bread to soak whatever condiment is on your plate, then proceed to eat the bread by bringing the fork to your mouth. The idea that it is okay to tear bread with the hands and dunk it into a bowl of gravy, then shoving the gravy-laden bread in your mouth with your hands is simply ludicrous. Not even the pets that reside in your home should witness this sort of creature-like behavior. You've probably done it before, but I forgive you. Let's start over!

Soups & Stews

For the avid soup lovers out there, there isn't another book that you need to read to learn all of the etiquette practices that should be followed when eating some good soup! One pet peeve which seems to be repetitive is that annoying little slurping sound that seems to follow soup wherever it goes! You know, that sound of a liquid being vacuumed into a dark abyss? Yep, that's the sound. Another famous one is of a hypnotized tongue continuously licking a now sparkling spoon. And let us not forget the scraping on the bowl when the soup is gone. Let's face it, I could definitely go on for days! But let's get down to business.

Here are a few tips to remember while eating soup:

- Always spoon soup away from you to allow the soup to trickle back in the bowl. This will avoid getting any soup on your shirt or lap!

- If the soup is too hot, stir it, don't blow and make that weird fan sound. Not only are you vigorously breathing over your meal, but it may come across that you are impatient and trying to rush the meal. I know, that may seem extreme, but others may perceive it that way.

- Always sip (never slurp) from the side of the spoon that faces you and never lean over the bowl while eating.

- When you have finished eating or wish to pause for a while, you can leave the spoon in the bowl if it is shallow, however, in the event that the bowl is deep or the soup is in a cup, you should place the spoon on the underplot or a saucer.

- If your soup contains noodles, it is ok to cut the noodles with the edge of your spoon to create bite sized pieces.

- If you desire a bite of bread to accompany your soup, it is not an acceptable etiquette practice to take the bread in one hand while holding the soupspoon in the other. The proper order would be to rest the spoon on your saucer then proceed to take a bite of the bread.

The proper way to hold a soup spoon is to gently rest the handle of the utensil on your middle finger, with your thumb firmly placed atop the spoon. You should always dip the spoon in a side way manner into the soup bowl, and try to avoid simply plopping the spoon deep down into the bowl to avoid spills and burns. So now that you've enjoyed your lovely soup and are approaching the bottom of the bowl and your unruly mouth is just watering to retrieve that last bit, but you're not too sure how to. It's totally within bounds to tilt the bowl and retrieve the last spoonful. Simple isn't it?

Eating French Onion Soup

For most individuals, mastering the art of eating French onion soup in public is a pretty scary thought, and so, to avoid the technicalities associated with eating a meal of this complexity we generally tend to avoid it, even if we like it and would love to have it. Well, that ends now! Tacking this soup may prove a tad bit tricky because it is topped with a slice of French bread which is generally covered with cheese. This makes it necessary to break through the cheesy "toast" before we can actually get down into the onion soup which lies below. So to proceed, take your spoon and in a gentle scraping motion remove the cheese from the top of the bread. Then, you may use the spoon and knife which is provided to cut your bread, you may eat the cheese and bread together or have the bread alone, after which you may incorporate the cheese into the actual soup and consume.

Frequently Asked Question

Question: I love incorporating crackers into my soup, are there rules associated with how they should be added during the dining experience?

Answer: There is actually an appropriate way of incorporating crackers into your soup. It is recommended that you add two or three oyster crackers at a time or you can crumble one saltine cracker into your bowl. Then, place the rest of your crackers on your bread plate. Sometimes soups tend to be on the thicker side, we definitely don't want to make it more difficult to eat or change its appearance to that of porridge.

Salad Etiquette

Okay, maybe eating salads is the least appalling of all the resentful mannerisms we have observed over the years from diners. Undoubtedly, some very nauseating habits are still heavily practiced today. These include but are not limited to: attempting to stuff an entire leaf of lettuce into the mouth all at once, opening the mouth as wide as a whale, or trying to eat a fork filled with croutons and delightful veggies. Let's just think about this from the perspective of an onlooker. Would you really want to be perceived in that light?

Here are some tips to follow when loading up on your favorite veggies:

- If there are a few pieces in your salad that are way too large, don't be afraid to cut them. When you are done cutting, place the knife across your butter plate with the blade facing you.

- In the event that you're against wasting food and desire to eat everything on your plate, always use your knife to push the food onto your fork, never your fingers. If you have a piece of bread, you may also use it to push food items onto your fork.

- When eating cherry tomatoes, depending on their size you may need to cut them. This can be simply achieved by sticking your fork into the larger cherry tomatoes then cutting them in half by virtue of the holes made. If they are small and able to fit into your mouth without you having to chew with your mouth open, feel free to do so.

American vs. Continental Style of Dining

Before you start eating your main course, it's very important for you to decide if you are going to use the American or Continental (European) Style of dining. I know, I know, you are probably thinking "who cares", or, "what is the American Style and Continental Style of dining". Well, if you plan to travel around the world, it's very important to know both styles. Additionally, both styles are correct; just make sure that you are consistent in its use.

American Style

The American Style of dining is commonly used by Americans and Canadians. This style is great to use when you want to take your time and really engage with those dining with you.

To use the American style of dining, follow these steps:

1. Cut one bite of your food with your fork and knife. If you are right-handed, your fork should be in your left hand, and your knife should be in your right hand. Although it's tempting, you should never use the side of your fork to cut.

2. After the knife is used to cut the food, place it on top of the plate with the blade facing in and then switch your fork to the right hand (or left hand if you cut with your left).

3. Pick up your food with your fork with the tines facing upwards.

4. Take a bite and repeat steps 1-3. The most stylish diners repeat this process with every bite, I'm not kidding!

It is important to note that the left hand should be placed in your lap, and should not be seen again until it is needed to cut the food. This style of dining is often referred to as the "zig zag" method, since the fork is constantly moving from the left to the right hand throughout the dining experience.

While we are on the topic of cutting, it's important to go through

Continental Style

A few years ago, I vividly remember dining with a friend from Corsica, which is an island in the Mediterranean Sea belonging to France. While eating, I realized that he was looking at me in a pretty strange manner. I simply asked him why he was staring at me like that, and that's when he made fun of how I was cutting my food; I was using the American Style of dining. He said that he wasn't familiar with that style, and it was in that moment that I decided it was time for me to master the Continental Style of dining.

The Continental Style is becoming more and more popular and even fashionable among diners. For all the adventurers and lovers of travel, this style should be utilized during your travels. This method is known as being the more graceful way of eating of the two. Basically, the first part of the Continental Style of dining is very similar to that of the American, but instead of switching hands, you would keep your fork in your right hand and your knife in your left hand. When you bring your food to your mouth with your fork, the tines should be facing downward.

When dining Continental Style, always remember that your knife and fork should be used together in unison, they simply do not work without the support of each other. It is important to completely avoid placing your fingers on the plate at any point in time, instead, employ the use of the knife to gently place food items on the fork. In this style of dining, both hands remain above the table as opposed to its American counterpart, and wrists should be placed at the edge of the table.

For both styles, remember, once you use your utensils, they should never touch the table again.

On the next page are the resting positions for when you want to give your jaws a rest:

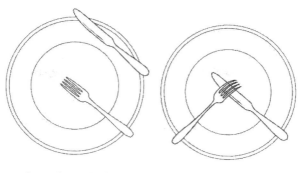

**American Style
Resting Position**

**Continental Style
Resting Position**

<u>Frequently Asked Question</u>

Question: I was recently told that I do not hold my utensils the correct way. Does it matter how I hold my utensils?

Answer: ABSOLUTELY! To be honest, you could probably get away with not knowing the two styles of dining, but you cannot get away with improperly holding your utensils. Below is the correct way to hold your utensils; which should be used for both the American and Continental style of dining.

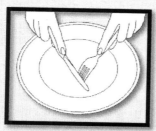

The Main Course

After being exposed to the proper way to break bread and the intricacies concerning eating various types of soups, it is now time for the main course! Whether you are a vegetarian or just a regular carnivore like the rest of the world, being able to properly use your utensils during your meal is vital for your survival in the dining world! So, after learning of the American and Continental styles of dining, this is your opportunity to show off those fancy finger works to your guests, who knows? You might even end up teaching other diners a thing or two.

For my meat eaters.....

Never cut up all your food before you eat, you're not a Gerber baby! You should always cut your food into bite sized pieces as you go along, embrace the experience. Remember, cut one to two pieces at a time. When served the half duck or chicken, use your knife and fork to cut away the wing and leg from the breast before you start eating any of the meat.

For my pasta lovers.....

You may be at odds as to whether you should cut your pasta or wind it up on your fork, to your surprise, both are acceptable, so go get your pasta on..... under certain circumstances! In the event that you are served thin noodles, similar to the ramen type, you should wound the noodles around the fork. If your meal is served with a spoon in the bowl, the purpose of the spoon is to use it as a leverage to getting the noodles onto the fork, whilst twirling the fork. If you are not presented with a spoon, it is not necessary to request one, you may simply leverage your noodles between the fork and the plate. When thick noodles are served, it is recommended that they be cut before you attempt to eat them.

The above mentioned entrees are generally what diners tend to order; hence their relevance to the etiquette discussion. But there's no need to worry, I won't continue with a long list of how to eat every item on the menu, that is certainly not necessary, you know how to eat broccoli in public..... I hope, with your fork right? Not fingers!

Many individuals have asked me if it is okay to eat with their fingers when they order French fries or if they're required to eat them with a fork, the answer is pretty simple; it depends on the setting. Here's the rule of thumb: if your main course requires the use of a knife and fork, it is only natural that you approach your side dish with the same finesse.

Unforeseen Circumstances

Although the way you eat during the meal is quite important, your attitude and mannerisms during those moments when you aren't actually eating will also be observed by your dinner party. Below are six unforeseen circumstances that could occur during your meal:

- If your meal isn't presented the way you've ordered it, it's perfectly fine to inform the server. Just make sure that you are discreet and please don't make a scene.

- If your glass, plate, or utensil is unclean, never use your napkin to wipe off smudges or dirt marks from the item. You should ask your server for a replacement and refrain from announcing it to your dinner party.

- If you drop a utensil on the ground or anything similar for that matter, it is inappropriate to pick it up from the ground and place it on the table. Consider that the floor is a melting pot of germs and bacteria, where individuals from all over the country have walked and brought dirt, mud, and grime from wherever they have trod (this is not to say that the restaurant is not well maintained). So, just leave the utensil there in all its glory and ask your server for a replacement. The only exception in this case is where the dropped utensil might endanger a passer-by or cause an accident if they were to step on it. In this regard, pick it up quickly, give the utensil to a server, and proceed to the restroom to wash and sanitize your hands.

- If someone at your table has a marinara mustache on his face, subtly grab his attention by dabbing your napkin on your chin or upper lip to signal to him where the food is located.

- If there is a strand of hair in your soup, as hard as this may be, try to avoid any conflict and fuss with other restaurant employees. Discretely gain the attention of a server and explain the issue. It is the norm that they would respond in a speedy manner, with either a replacement or a new plate of your choice. When these unfortunate situations occur, the restaurant usually waives the cost of your bill or throws in a few of their spectacular dishes for free. Although accidents do happen, it is your duty to handle yourself in a professional manner and not lower your standards - although you might be pretty enraged.

- If something that tastes funky or foul ends up in your mouth (ex. a piece of fat), you can raise your fork to your mouth and subtly use your tongue to remove the object from your mouth and place it on your fork. (Easy rule: If it went in with a utensil, it comes out on a utensil.) Then place the item to the side of your plate. Never place or directly spit an item into your napkin! You may also excuse yourself to the restroom and remove the unpleasant bite that you think would be offensive or even distracting if removed at the table. Please make sure you practice this technique before you apply it while dining with others; I would hate for that undesirable item to end up in your lap.

These are just a few of the unforeseen circumstances that could occur during your meal and there are many more that could occur. Just remember to be discrete and never make a scene, if you follow those tips I know you will be in good shape!

Is There Really a Right Way to Share Food?

Since we're discussing the main meal, let's take this opportunity to share a few hints on what essentially led to me becoming the queen of etiquette I am today. During my childhood, my household went to dinner 3-4 times per week, and so, from a very tender age I became quite aware of both my parents' and my pet peeves while dining. One rule in particular which was central to our dinner experiences was that we should order what we want. Period. For example, if my dad asked us, "Does anyone want salad?" and we all say no, we can't then ask to taste his salad. He would definitely give us a side eye capable of making your entire skeletal system tremble. His motto was simple yet powerful, "Order what you want.". So, if any of you ever dine with my dad, just forget about asking to taste his food. However, here are some simple guidelines to follow when sharing food:

- Never ask to taste someone's food before they taste it. I mean, just think about that, isn't that just extremely distasteful? If you must, allow the person to enjoy the food they ordered first before asking for a taste. If you can avoid asking, that would be more desirable.

- If you want to try someone's food, you must surely be courteous enough to ask first. Also, give them the opportunity to answer you, it's rude to just ask and grab.

- Never take advantage of the offerors generosity. If you ask to taste fries for example, take 2-3, don't attempt to take a handful.

- When eating nachos, never try to stack all of the meat on each nacho that you pick up. Also, it's quite inappropriate to touch every nacho before finally choosing one; and double dipping is a definite no-no.

From the various ways of eating different foods to navigating the unforeseeable circumstances which may arise during the dining experience, it is always noteworthy to remember the reasons for dining, and although they may be different across cultures and countries, one undeniable constant is the enjoyment of the company of family and friends.

The End of the Meal

You've finished your scrumptious meal, and now you are ready for your server to whisk away your plate! Let's just be honest here, how many of you have ever pushed back your plate? Or even announced to the dinner party "I'm stuffed!" and then rolled down in your seat and rubbed your belly?

Here are a few things you should never do when you're finished eating your main course:

- Never put your utensils back on the table. Rule of thumb: Once you use your utensils, they should never touch the table again. Imagine the table is draped in a white linen tablecloth, do you really think that it would be appropriate to place your used steak knife back on the table? I think not.

- Never slouch back in your chair and announce to the table that you are done eating.

- Never pull out your cell phone to check the time or engage in other activities.

- Never put your beautiful linen napkin on your plate. It should be neatly placed on the left side of your setting. If you are ordering dessert, keep your napkin on your lap.

- Never push your plate away from you. You can signal to your seerver that you are done by putting your utensils in the "I'm done" position as shown below.

**American Style
Finished Position**

**Continental Style
Finished Position**

Pretty often, individuals get nervous about asking for a doggy bag after they have finished eating. I would like to declare that there is absolutely nothing wrong with requesting one. However, in instances where you are on a date or having lunch over a business meeting, this is not recommended.

Often in upscale restaurants, the server may bring over steam-moistened towelettes at the end of the meal. These should be used to wipe your hands and if necessary, used to gently dab the area around your mouth. When you are done the server will either promptly retrieve them, but if not, it is definitely okay to rest it atop the loosely folded napkin to the side of your plate.

If you still have room for dessert, keep these rules in mind:

- If you are dining with a group and the host doesn't order dessert, you probably shouldn't proceed to order for yourself. Furthermore, if you are the only one from your dinner party interested in ordering dessert, you should avoid proceeding because the entire party will have to wait an extra 20 minutes to receive the bill because of your decision to order.

- After the completion of dinner and removal of your plate, your dessert spoon and fork may be moved to the left and right of your place setting. When eating dessert a la mode such as apple pie for instance, it is proper to do so with both fork and spoon. The fork should be held in your right hand, while the spoon should be held in your left and used to push additions such as whipped cream and ice cream onto your forkful of pie.

So, you've finally made it to the end of the guideline on dining in a restaurant, but pump your breaks; you can't just storm off. Remember that tantalizing meal you just ingested, you have to pay for it!

Here are a few etiquette tips as it relates to handling the check:

- If you are with a group and you are paying for the bill, let the server know beforehand. This avoids the "no, I insist on paying for the meal" conversation and going back and forth. If you forget to let the server know, no big deal. Just make sure that when the server places the check on the table, you grab it immediately. This will indicate that you are paying for the bill.

- If you are with a group and everyone is paying separately, you should always let your server know before you place your order. This way, they can separate the orders in the beginning instead of doing it at the end. This is also important because the restaurant may not accept multiple payments from the same table. I recommend calling the restaurant beforehand to make sure that they will accept separated payments.

- If there is a problem with the bill, quietly discuss it with your server. If your server is uncooperative, excuse yourself from the table and ask to speak to the manager in efforts to resolve the issues you may have. Don't be scared or intimidated by the thought of inquiring, you have that right, even if the bill turns out to be correct at the end of the inquiry, at least you will have a clearer understanding of why it costed as much as it did.

- Always tip your server, and I'm not referring to the old crumbled one dollar that has gone to hell and back; give a decent tip for the services rendered- this is usually around 20%.

- If you order one plate and share it between yourself and another, be sure to tip the waiter for two plates as opposed to one.

Frequently Asked Question

Question: What should I do if my credit card declines?

Answer: Unfortunately, this has happened to me before! There was a fraud alert because I spent half the day out with girlfriends shopping, and my credit card company was like "whooa hold on! Leontina doesn't spend that much on items in one day". I was embarrassed and didn't know what to do. I knew that I had money in the bank, so instead of making a fuss with my server, I just asked my friend if I could pay her back. Now, when I called the credit company, I wasn't as nice!

Here are the steps you should take if your credit card declines and you know that you are not over your limit:

- Do not call attention to the situation.

- If your card continues to be declined, and you do not have enough cash to pay, ask to pay by check, visit the nearest ATM, or return the next day with cash.

- If the restaurant declines these suggestions, you have no option but to return to the table and throw yourself on the mercy of your companions. Repay their kindness within 24 hours, repaying them in cash.

So, the amazing meal surrounded by great company has come to an end, you've dealt with your bill and now you might not be so sure on what to do. The last tip as it relates to dining out is that you should always thank your host. However, in the event that you are the host, go ahead and thank your guests for choosing to spend their quality time with you, appreciation is always appreciated!

Dinner Party Etiquette

Having explored dining etiquette from start to finish in a restaurant setting, I thought it would be important to provide guidance for other dining settings. I really want you to feel extremely comfortable, even if that means dining on the moon. So let's get to it!

In this chapter we will discuss the roles of both host and guest, and what they entail with regard to a dinner party setting. Some people might not consider this to be a big deal, but it is quite important that each individual has the ability to easily and comfortably use any place setting, regardless of how simple and casual it may appear or whether it is fancy and visually appealing. This is because, regardless of the fact that it may be in another person's home, you still risk embarrassment when you are unsure of how to actually conduct yourself at the dining table. Furthermore, your embarrassment might actually be substantial, but when you consider that of your host who invited you to dine around other people, they may also feel uneasy by your actions.

Let's examine the role of the host and the considerations which should be made when hosting a dinner party.

Menu
The menu is by far the most important aspect of having a well put together dinner party. Whether you intend for the event to be formal or informal, people come with the intention to eat, so it is necessary to have a well-

rounded menu with items suitable for just about anyone. In my amateur days, the old Leontina wouldn't serve spicy food at her dinner parties because that isn't what I liked. But having matured and outgrown the idea that the sun, moon and stars revolve around me, I have come to assume a more humble approach. If you are in fact inviting guests over, it should be your primary consideration to provide food to their liking that they would actually want to eat.

Also, when you are forming your menu, keep seasons in mind; so if it is really hot outside, your guests probably wouldn't want hot beverages like tea or want to have a hot soup for an appetizer. A more suitable choice for your summertime fling might actually be light refreshing foods that are in season.

Counter space and eating space is also pretty important. I bought my first condo at the age of twenty-four, and within the first month I planned my first dinner party and was ambitious enough to have a total of seven dishes. Unfortunately, this took up all of my counter space and I had to place some dishes on the dining table; there was little room for my guest to eat, talk about a disaster. So, the moral of the story is to consider counter space as you are thinking about the menu.

Greeting Your Guests

When you invite guests over, you should always meet them at the door. Never allow your guests to come searching through your house to greet you, that's a clear display of poor manners and a sure way to make your guests uncomfortable within a short period of entering your home. Immediately take coats and jackets from your guests, and you may ask a close family member or friend who has helped you in the preparation for the party to assist you in hanging the coats in another room.

As soon as your guests arrive, it's important to give instructions regarding food and drinks and also introduce your guests to friends and family members who have already arrived. When the majority of your guests have arrived, briefly walk around to ensure that everyone is comfortable in the space and ensure that you have enough food and drinks for everyone to be satisfied throughout the party.

Serving cocktails before the commencement of dinner is a great way to allow your prompt guests to socialize with others while you await the arrival of the other guests. Cocktail hour should be no longer than an hour before the start of dinner, and as with the food menu, you should consider serving a wide range of beverages, remembering that not everyone consumes alcohol. Finger foods may also be served with the cocktails, but their flavour and cuisine should be similar to the main course.

Serving Wine

It is customary to serve the choice of wine with dinner. However, this, as with everything else in this book requires some expertise. The wine should be suitably paired with the entree being served at dinner. Generally speaking, white wines are served with fish, chicken, lamb and veal; while red wines are served with beef, some forms of poultry (such as cornish hens) and pastas with a red sauce. If you are unsure of what wines would best accompany your menu, feel free to stop by a wine shop and get expert advice from consultants there.

Here are a few pointers regarding the serving of wine:

- Wine glasses should only be filled halfway, you should never fill to the top of the glass! As previously mentioned, each wine is to have its own glass, furthermore, the glasses should be clean and spotless, there is nothing more unappetizing than being given a wine glass smudged with fingerprints.

- Red wine should always be served at room temperature, and should never be refrigerated. Once the bottle is opened, the wine should be allowed about 30 minutes to develop in scent and flavour before being served.

- Red wine should be served in wine glasses with a big bowl, this is to facilitate the drinker being able to smell the developed bouquet aroma of the wine, and consequently result in the increased taste.

- White wines should always be served chilled, but under no circumstance should they be placed in the freezer to chill, this is quite dangerous as the glass bottle could crystallize and break, and this could potentially hide the authentic taste of the wine and make it less appealing.

- White wines are also intentionally served in smaller wine glasses when compared to red wine glasses, this is because they should be held at the stem and not the bowl. Our fingertips tend to transfer warmth to things we touch, and touching the bowl of a white wine glass would certainly warm the wine.

Serving Dinner

Planning an elegant dinner party may be moderately rated on the difficulty scale, however, with a few hints and tips, you will be able to master the requirements in no time.

- If your dinner party is of a formal nature, be sure to have your table set before your guests arrive, you may refer back to chapter three for guidelines on creating various settings.

- Always announce that dinner is ready and lead your guests to the dining room.

- Some of your guests may have read this book, and they will instinctively know that they should not remove their napkin from the table until their host has been seated and done so. If you are the host, it is important to act promptly and put your napkin on your lap to indicate that it is time to eat, or you may simply offer your guests permission to dig in.

- In the event that you are hosting an informal dinner party, ensure that each dish is accompanied by a serving spoon and large fork for the guests to serve themselves.

- Instead of having condiments in individual containers, it would be wise to have at least two divided containers for condiments; depending on the number of guests.

- When everyone has been served, it is advisable to place foods which should be served warm into the oven until a second serving is requested.

Now that dinner has ended and you are satisfied to the point where you're ready to catch a quick nap, just put that wonderful idea on hold; because it's time to clean up!

Cleaning Up

It is the norm for guests to ask if you need help with clean up after dinner, you should always thank them for offering, but you should never say yes. Before dinner begins, you should have at least two individuals specially designated to assist you with cleaning up prior to dinner.

The Roles of the Guest

Have you ever attended a dinner party, only to have your patience and lip service tested by that one person who simply feels the need to dominate conversation; or simply thinks that it is okay to have other individuals tag along without the permission of the host?

Below are a few tips to keep in mind when you are a guest:

- Always bring a gift for your host, this may be something as simple as a fragrant candle, or even a bottle of wine to share over dinner.

- Feel free to mingle with the other guests and introduce yourself.

- If you spill something before the start of dinner, be sure to let your host know so that it can be cleaned up immediately. If however, you damage something, you are responsible for paying for the damage.

- Never bring an uninvited guest unless you have first received permission from the host.

- The majority of informal dinner parties are served family style. With that being said, dishes should always be passed around the table in a counter-clockwise manner; additionally, when salad is being served in family style dining, it is usually passed in a large bowl from guest to guest. When you are passing food around, you should always hold it for the person to your right.

- When dining family style, it is recommended that you wait until at least three individuals have been served before proceeding to eat. This is simply because the process of passing and sharing meals may be time consuming and it would be rather inconsiderate to allow all guests to wait until such process has ended. If you are in fact hosting, be sure to communicate this information to your guests.

When conversing with others before and after dinner, it is necessary to make the conversation light and friendly, this will ensure that others are interested in and may be included in the discussion. It is absolutely important to refrain from speaking on topics that are in any way limiting, and will prevent others from being able to actively participate. It is recommended that topics that tend to stimulate laughter and cause persons to feel comfortable are selected. Make it a point of duty to speak to persons sitting closest to you and not those further away from you.

Let me tell you a quick story: my friends call me the Networking Queen because I can go to an event and leave with ten new best friends! They generally ask me how I achieve this and there is a craft to meeting new people without seeming awkward or uncomfortable. Here are my three best conversation starters for dinner parties:

- Start by complimenting the other individual on something they are wearing, this could be shoes, a purse, a suit or any other visible item. However, don't stop there when they say "thank you"; ask them where they got it or tell them that you've been looking for a similar item.

- Ask them how often they have known the host. In the event that they say they know them from work, ask them about their profession and take the conversation from there.

- Ask about the area in which the individual lives (not their specific address), from there you may follow up with a question such as "are there good restaurants in the area?" and go on to mention that you are interested in trying new places to eat.

There may be instances where you may be interested in exiting the conversation, below are ways in which you can tactfully leave the conversation in an acceptable way:

- You may offer to refill their drink; in the event that they say yes, you may simply deliver the beverage and carry on.

- You may say, "I'm so sorry, please excuse me. Do you know where the restroom is?"

- You may say, "I am dying to try that bruschetta! Would you please excuse me?"

- You may say, "Please excuse me, I told the babysitter that I'd check in at this time. Please excuse me."

- You may say, "It's been so nice talking to you, let's chat later!"

- You may say, "There's my friend Sam. Have you met him?" You may then proceed to include Sam in the conversation and then exit with one of the comments above.

With all of the above information, you will be more than ready to perfectly perform the role of either a model host or guest. Do not be dissuaded by the seemingly hard aspects of performing either role, be confident in your abilities and practice, practice, practice! Before you know it, you too could be teaching etiquette practices and writing books to demonstrate the importance of dining etiquette.

Buffet Etiquette

So, here we are at the second to last chapter of the book, and what better topic to discuss than buffet etiquette. Whether you are at a regular paid food bouquet or an event such as a wedding, there are certain rules and regulations which govern the food stations at these locations.

I've never been germ phobic, so usually I'm not too disgusted by buffets. However, with the behaviours I've been witnessing lately, especially those in close proximity to the buffet line, I can't help but cringe. For some reason, people think that because buffets are casual settings, the golden rules of dining etiquette have somehow vanished into the great abyss. But I am here to reinforce that etiquette spans all dining experiences and much more. Let's take a look at buffet etiquette.

Buffet Etiquette

As previously mentioned, I used to love buffets! My favorite was Old Country Buffet. I know I probably shouldn't name drop, but they had the best ice cream cones ever! Here are some rules to follow while at the buffet counter:

- Scout the buffet line before actually choosing what you want. Let's face it, a stacked plate is a recipe for embarrassment, and we don't want to be judged!

- Never bring a used plate to the buffet line, that is unsanitary and it will certainly lead to the spread of germs. Always get a new plate.

- Never reach around someone to get the food, that's plain rude!

- Never touch the food with your fingers.

- Always place the serving utensils back into their respective dishes to avoid cross contamination. This is one tip that is near and dear to my heart as my mom is allergic to certain foods.

- If you feel the urge to sneeze or cough, always move away from the table as quickly as possible and turn your body away from the buffet line.

- Unlike formal and informal dinners, you do not have to wait for everyone to be seated to start eating.

- Never ask for a doggie bag.

Frequently Asked Questions

Question: Do I have to leave a tip?

Answer: Absolutely! Be reminded that the staff has to remove your dirty plates and clean your table. Also, at most places, they are responsible.

Hosting a Buffet Dinner

Hosting a buffet can be a great stress-free way to allow your guests to mix and mingle, while providing guests easy access to foods from multiple angles. Below are a few tips on hosting a buffet, followed by the roles of guests at a buffet.

- A great way to avoid the onset of confusion is to have specific items located at particular stations so as to prevent a floodgate of guests when dinner is served. The items may be separated by courses or otherwise.

- Although you may already have tables set in anticipation of guests, it is important to have additional plates and utensils in the event that your guests desire a second serving.

- Keep lots of napkins and hand towels on hand in case of spills and small messes.

- In the event that you have ice cream at the dessert station, be sure to keep it in the freezer until the appropriate serving time. It is also a good idea to place it in a container with ice to prevent the ice cream from melting.

- Use an ice bucket with tongs to prevent individuals from using their hands.

Roles of a Buffet Guest

- Only take items that you know you will eat. If you're still desirous after you have finished, you may take a new plate to the buffet line, after first servings have been completed, to get a second serving.

- Always offer to assist a person you know, when you see someone having trouble balancing a plate or pouring a drink. However, I would not recommend asking a complete stranger.

- Having children around hot food and breakable items is never a good idea. It is recommended that children be served and seated first to avoid any accidents, after which adults may be served.

- In the event that you bring your children along, remember that they are your responsibility and that it is for you to oversee their activities.

Having gone through the various roles of host and guest, go on with your bad self and demonstrate your mastery of buffet settings. Don't forget to tell them that Leontina taught you!

Fast Food Etiquette

With fast food restaurants located on every block, and sometimes right beside one another, you should really expect that I would have a thing or two to say about how we conduct ourselves in these places. Let's face it, we live in a fast paced world and singles and families are often strapped for time. This is where the amazing "fast" food comes to the rescue, and although we may feel incredibly sinful after indulging in something with the caloric value of a cow, we like how it tastes and we feel good about eating it! With that said, we may be more relaxed in these establishments and have zero care for how people actually think of the way we dine there, but the point I'm trying to get at is that at one point or another, we have all experienced something disturbing, and by forgetting the rules of etiquette, we are simply continuing the cycle.

Pretty often I get the comment: "I don't need to demonstrate etiquette at McDonalds!" which actually, is pretty false! In this section I will go through a few mannerisms that should be observed in the drive-thru and within the establishment.

- Never order at the drive-thru then change your order at the payment window, not only does this increase the wait time for other buyers who literally intended to just drive-thru, you may even cause the employees to become confused about the orders which have already been taken.

- You should enter the drive-thru with the intention of actually ordering and not just figuring out what you want at the expense of other eager purchasers.

- In the event that your order is complex and requires various modifications, do order inside the establishment. Not only will this cut down on the time spent holding up the line while you make the special order, it will also allow you to check your purchase thoroughly on the inside, where others can actually pass you.

- If there are multiple people in your vehicle with separate orders and they each plan to pay individually, it would be best to order inside.

- Always have your cash out and ready to pay.

- Turn your music down

For the drive-thru establishments that have two lines, sometimes it may be difficult to tell when it is your turn to go. However, it is never okay to honk your horn and yell at the car in front of you. Always stay calm and polite while you are going through the drive-thru.

> ## **Frequently Asked Questions**
>
> **Question:** Is there a correct way to place a special food order?
>
> **Answer:** Yes, There is a way to make a specialized food order. Let's say for instance, you want to order a cheeseburger without onions. The appropriate way to make this order would be to say, "I'd like to order a cheeseburger with no onions or ketchup, a large shake, and an apple pie." You should never say, "I'd like to order a cheeseburger, a large shake, and an apple pie – and oh yea, no ketchup or onions on the cheeseburger". The appropriate way to place a special order is to tell staff what you want changed as soon as you order that item, as opposed to at the end of the order. By doing this, the person taking your order will not have to go back and delete an item.

Dining Inside

The convenience of fast food restaurants can be quite tempting, but there is no reason on Earth why a quick bite to eat should turn into a terrible dining experience. Additionally, kids should not be gallivanting around the dining room while others are simply trying to eat their food. Such behaviour should be confined to the play area, and the designated play area only! Furthermore, if you're unsure of what to order, do not step up to the counter and begin perusing the menu, wait until you have decided what to purchase. Below are a few more fast food etiquette tips while dining in:

- Never allow your child to pay for their kids meal with the coins from their piggy bank. Counting out seven dollars in pennies is sure to drive other consumers crazy!

- If you received your order and it is wrong, don't assume that it is the cashiers fault and jump to blaming him/her.

- If you spill something, be sure to tell an employee right away to prevent accidents from occurring.

- Be sure to clean up after yourself. Restaurants can get very busy and there might not always be a designated employee for the cleaning of tables. Leave it in the condition you would like to use it.

- Never allow your children to run around, this isn't in the best interest of their safety and may potentially cause unintended harm to others.

- Always say please and thank you to individuals you come into contact with; especially the cashiers.

- Never waste condiments and napkins. Although you may not care about the money the restaurant has to spend to pay for the unused condiments, consider one factor which we are all affected by; that is the environment. Only take what you need, this will diminish waste.

Dining etiquette isn't simply about doing things properly or in a way stipulated to be exercised; this form of etiquette is actually a sign of respect and honor which is displayed through your mannerisms, and is indicative of your care and appreciation of everyone from the farmer to the person that empties the trash after you're done eating. Don't think of it as an outward facade that you must master and study. Simply consider it to be an outward sign of the inner-respect that you possess for the food and the people who prepare it!

***

So, you did it! You made it to the end of this amazing book, and I sure do hope that you have laughed, been pleasantly surprised, and certainly learned quite a bit about dining etiquette in formal and informal situations! Dining etiquette is a journey, so remember, you can't learn it all in one night. If you really dig deep and stay determined to master the art of dining etiquette, I assure you that the grace and gentle demeanor with which you conduct yourself when dining will cause rave reviews, and sooner or later you won't have to worry about embarrassing yourself!

Now the ball is in your court; you have all the basic tools which you need for success! So, go make that reservation and call up a few friends! It's time to dine.

For corporate bookings, executive education, and
media relations, please visit
<u>www.steppingintoetiquette.com</u>

Made in the USA
Middletown, DE
04 May 2019